HOW TO EXCEL IN RETIREMENT

SO THAT YOU CAN LIVE WORRY-FREE

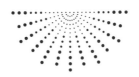

DAVID C. TREECE

Copyright © 2024 by David C. Treece

All rights reserved.

No part of this book may be reproduced in any form or by any electronic or mechanical means, including information storage and retrieval systems, without written permission from the author, except for the use of brief quotations in a book review.

*This book is dedicated to
Mallory who believed in me before I did.*

*Special thanks to
Abby Minihan for the cover design and
Michael LaRocca who has edited my writing for more than 10 years.*

CONTENTS

Contact & Disclosure	vii
Preface	ix
1. Do You Have a Plan?	1
2. Social Security Simplified: Details and what to look out for	5
3. What Is a Sustainable Withdrawal Rate?	9
4. How Times Are Changing	12
5. The Three Roles of Money and Specifics on Investments	15
6. Taxes and Using Roth IRAs	27
7. What Else Can We Do to Save on Taxes?	31
8. What To Do When the Stock Market is Down	33
9. Let's Talk About QCDs	34
10. Here's Another Tax Efficiency Strategy	35
11. Let's Talk About Recent Legislative Changes	37
12. How to Pick a Financial Advisor	39
13. The Value of Independence	43
14. Conclusion	45
Endnotes	49
About the Author	53
Notes	55

CONTACT & DISCLOSURE

For more information, please contact:

> *David C. Treece, Financial Planner & Founder*
> *Clients Excel*
> *www.clientsexcel.com*
> *hello@clientsexcel.com*
> *864.641.7955*

Licensed Insurance Professional. We are an independent financial services firm helping individuals create retirement strategies using a variety of investment and insurance products to custom suit their needs and objectives. This material has been prepared for informational and educational purposes only. It is not intended to provide, and should not be relied upon for, accounting, legal, tax or investment advice.

Investing involves risk, including the loss of principal. No Investment strategy can guarantee a profit or protect against loss in a period of declining values. Any references to protection benefits or lifetime income generally refer to fixed insurance products, never securities or investment products. Insurance and annuity products are backed by the financial strength and claims-paying ability of the issuing insurance company.

PREFACE

Some of my earliest memories are from my parents' business. I've been around the financial services industry most of my life. My dad got into financial services in the mid-1980s right after I was born. My mom worked in his office for many years before she became too sick to work.

Work and family time blended together, and I heard countless conversations about my parents' business. Probably like a lot of small business, things could get stressful when figuring out how to best run the company. It felt like my parents were often stressed out.

When I got older, I wanted nothing to do with the business. But as I got to my late twenties, I started thinking about what settling down and having a family would look like for me. I remembered my dad always had time to take me hunting and fishing, and my mom had time to take me to Charlotte Hornets basketball games. Those are wonderful memories. I was fortunate to have the unique opportunity to observe how to run a financial services business. The wheels in my mind began turning. The financial services business sounded like a great way to make a living. With that epiphany, I started the licensing process.

Initially, I went to work for a financial professional who focused on home and car insurance, and I didn't get a lot of training or help to be successful. About a year into that position, I told my dad I was coming to work for him. I worked with him in his office in North Carolina, where I'm from, for almost six years.

During that time, I married my wife, Mallory. One of the best things I've done. She lived about a hundred miles south of me in South Carolina. She was a high school art teacher and had a nice house when we got married. So, I decided I'd do the hundred-mile drive back and forth to work a couple times a week. Oh, the things we do for love!

We had our first daughter in 2017, and it became increasingly difficult for me to be out of town after that. I left Dad's business in September 2018, and launched my own financial planning firm named Clients Excel where we focus on helping good people make wise financial decisions so that they may excel in retirement with confidence. I'll tell you more about that later in this guide.

Over the years, I've had the privilege of sitting with hundreds of people who were close to retirement or in retirement. I've seen what works for people, and I've seen some common pitfalls that I hope you'll be able to avoid by reading this book. From here, we'll talk about the steps you can take to help retire with precision, so that you can be as prepared as possible.

1

DO YOU HAVE A PLAN?

*S*ome people go into retirement with no plan and that can be risky.

When I was in my twenties I moved to Denver, Colorado. I love the outdoors, and the Western mountains are captivating. It's hard to have a bad day when you can look west and see huge mountains from almost anywhere. It's always a sight worth seeing.

Do you know that there are 58 mountain peaks[1] in Colorado that are 14,000 feet tall or more? I wanted to conquer as many as possible! It seemed like an adventure worth having. The hikes to the top of the "14ers," as they are commonly called, vary drastically. Some hikes are easy walk ups, some require precision, and some can be dangerous to traverse. The point is, they all have varying degrees of risk associated with them.

Before I moved to Colorado, I lived in Virginia where I went to college. While in school, I worked at a coffee shop, and I met one of my best friends while serving java. Chris and I had several common interests, and one of them was the outdoors. On a few occasions, we would be working together and decide during our shift that we would go camping that night somewhere in the Blue Ridge Mountains. We'd take off after work with a vague idea of where we were going. I'm glad my mom didn't know about my antics. She probably would have been worried sick.

We often hiked on the Appalachian Trail off the Blue Ridge Parkway. The Parkway was a short distance from town and easy to access. When we camped out on the trail, we would get up and make a camp breakfast that always included a hot cup of coffee. And it wasn't the instant kind found at some campsites. It was coffee worthy of being served in a gourmet shop.

After I moved to Colorado, Chris decided to come out one summer to work at a coffee shop in Denver. His plan was to enjoy a few months out west, then go back home to Virginia. Right before he was to leave to go home, he wanted to have one last adventure. He asked me if I'd hiked a 14er before, and at that point I had not. It seemed important to him to conquer a 14er before he left.

We asked another friend if he'd hiked any 14ers, and he said he'd hiked Mount of Holy Cross near Vail. Mount of the Holy Cross sounded good enough for us, so we planned a morning to make the hike. Chris came over to my apartment late the night before because he had to close the coffee shop. We did what most carefree 20-somethings do…We stayed up late getting our gear out and talking things through.

As it turns out, responsibly hiking a 14er takes careful planning. It's important to have your ascent complete by the time noon rolls around because the weather can quickly change at altitude. Even in the middle of the summer, it may snow, sleet or hail, or you may experience an afternoon windstorm. The conditions quickly can go from tranquil to dangerous. Hiking at elevation is to be respected or Mother Nature may have her way with you.

We got up early and started our two-hour drive to the trailhead. We were lackadaisical, but we were confident we'd be fine. After all, we had hiked extensively back east, and we were full of youthful ambition. We stopped at a fast food restaurant for a restroom break before navigating up the fire road to the trailhead. In the daylight, the dirt road up to the trail required careful concentration. Imagine what that drive would be like at night. If only we had that perspective starting out…

Once we got to the trailhead, we figured we needed one more jolt of caffeine. We pulled out the camp stove coffee maker and made coffee. I was beginning to sense the urgency, but I wasn't overly compelled to put our plans in high gear. Around ten that morning, we started our hike. Shortly into the hike we passed some hikers coming back. We asked how the hike was, and they used curse words as adjectives to explain the level of difficulty. We laughed it off and thought they must be novices. But internally, I was starting to worry.

Little did I know, we were in for a shock. We casually took our time. We stopped for pictures along the way with the mountain peak behind us. The last segment of elevation included large rocks to navigate up that required careful attention.

We finally summited Mount of Holy Cross around three in the afternoon. We knew we should probably turn around before summiting, but we were comforted by seeing two other sets of hikers doing the same thing. When we finally got to the top, we were exhausted. We were literally on top of the world and wanted to take it all in. As I sat there, I began to doze off. The altitude had exhausted me. At altitude your body works harder, and you fatigue quicker. After a few minutes, I looked over at Chris. He looked bad. Have you ever looked at someone and thought they just don't look right? Chris was out of water and he was severely dehydrated. Your body uses more water at altitude. Now, we had our first major problem.

We knew we had to be off the large rocks by dark at the latest. That was our first goal. When it became apparent that we would be in the woods well after dark, I began the mental deliberation of whether we should try to camp, but we had no camping supplies. We had one headlamp and very little food. We began melting snow to put in our water bottles to drink. We were in bad shape.

As dusk approached, I put the headlamp on and walked behind Chris as he put one foot in front of the other. If there was a turtle racing us, the turtle would have won. I tried encouraging Chris, but I knew things could get worse at any moment. It's hard to be positive in a time of crisis. I'm a problem solver, but I could not figure out a way to fix this issue. Plus, nothing looks the same at night in the woods. We finally got back to the Jeep around ten that night, and now I had the task of driving down the perilous fire road in the dark. After we got out to the interstate, I looked over at Chris and he was doubled over fast asleep.

Over the years I've been in the financial services business, I've found some people start off their retirement journey with hopeful ambition but few concrete plans. They decide they are ready to climb their retirement mountain, and they go off with nothing more than the anecdotal experiences from co-workers for family members. The problem with polling our family, co-workers and friends about retirement planning is we are all different. We have different work histories, health statuses, assets, and the list goes on. We are all unique, and we all have nuance to our lives. What makes you tick may not make your co-worker tick. Their anecdotal financial advice may not fit you. Individual planning is essential making sure you are positioned to achieve as many of your objectives as possible.

A 2024 finding from The National Council on Aging estimates that 17 million people over 65 are considered economically insecure."[2] That's a crisis! Now I know if you're reading this book, that may not be you. And that's a great thing. Perhaps in another book we can cover what folks who are underfunded for retirement should do. For the remainder of this book, we'll cover some of the practical steps you can take to help avoid pitfalls and improve your chances of excelling in retirement.

2

SOCIAL SECURITY SIMPLIFIED: DETAILS AND WHAT TO LOOK OUT FOR

The first step to figuring out if you should retire or if you can retire is to figure out the totality of your current budget needs. What I mean is: What does it take to pay your bills every month? If you're not a spreadsheet person, I encourage you to sit down with a pen and paper and your bank statement. Figure out where your money is going and what your income needs to be each month to live. Figure out what it takes to keep the lights on each month, then figure out what a livable budget is. Include eating out or going to the movies if you do those things.

I spent many days with my maternal grandparents as a kid. My grandfather was about twelve-years-old when the Great Depression started. He learned early on the value of a job, and after spending so much time with him I wanted to make him proud. Growing up in the Depression created the worldview inside my grandfather that having a job was a virtue, and it was a highly esteemed attribute. That influence led me to want a job as soon as I was old enough to work. When I turned fifteen, I got a job working in the kitchen of a seafood restaurant making minimum wage. I remember my grandfather being so proud that I was gainfully employed. Ever since that first job, I've been paying into Social Security. If you're like many of the people I sit down with, you've heard that Social Security may not be there for you when you are retired.

It's no conspiracy. For many years now, the Social Security Administration has stated[1] that by the 2030s, they will no longer be able to pay all the scheduled benefits. As of 2023, the Social Security Board of Trustees Report stated that there is enough money to fund full benefits until 2033. After that, the report states the government will be able to fund 77 cents for every dollar of scheduled benefits.[2] Now is the time for Congress to figure out a solution, not years down the road when the deadline is more imminent.

The next question we have to ask ourselves is, will Social Security be enough? According to Social Security, the program is only designed to cover 40% of our income needed in retirement.[3]

Ida Mae Fuller, a legal secretary from Vermont, was the first recipient[4] of Social Security in 1940 at age 65. She collected $22.54 in benefits per month. She paid $24.75 into the program. In 1940 women were only expected to live[5] until 65, but she lived to 100. She received $22,888.92 in Social Security benefits. Talk about a win! I think she blew up the actuarial tables. The program was not originally intended for everyone to have the opportunity to claim Social Security. When most everyone is claiming benefits, it strains the program. You would think that by this point we would have figured out a solution to this problem, but we haven't.

When claiming Social Security, it's important to be cognizant of the program's lack of funding, but I don't think making decisions based on fear is healthy. We want to be informed but not fearful. Unfortunately, fear is often a reason people act one way or another. Statistically, most people claim their benefits as soon as they can at age 62, but we would be wise to remember that by doing so we are giving up 8% per year of "delayed retirement credits."[6]

According to the Social Security Administration[7], "Nearly 90% of Americans ages 65 and older received Social Security benefits as of the end of 2022." And, the average benefit across the country is $1,825 per month, but benefits vary greatly. Currently, benefit payouts top out around $3,627 per month. So where do you turn for advice on Social Security benefits?

In our financial advisory practice, we believe proper Social Security planning is so important that we conduct at least half a dozen informational seminars every year on the subject. We take a deep dive into what the Social Security program is and how to optimize your benefits so they work best for you.

We've been paying into Social Security since we began working, so it only makes sense to want to get the most out of our benefits. If we call the Social Security Administration and ask for advice, they won't give it to us. Unfortunately, the Administration is not equipped to provide advice for your unique situation. They will answer your specific questions if you know what to ask. But in life, knowing the right questions to ask is often the biggest challenge.

You'll need to find a dedicated advisor who is well equipped to help you get the most out of your benefits. It's no exaggeration that making the wrong decision can be costly. The software we use in our office reveals that often there is over $100,000 (sometimes more) in play with how and when we claim Social Security, yet most people claim without knowing all the details that affect them. Even if you plan to claim at 62, wouldn't you want to know all the details of what's at stake before you decide? I'm guessing you probably do if you're still reading. I like knowing all the details before I make a major decision. I don't think we can make a well-informed decision without knowing the details.

The steps to figuring out when to claim Social Security have several variables. We've mentioned our expenses. Figuring out what money we need per month is step one. We can know what our benefits are from our statement by downloading it at SSA.gov. Then, we have to consider our life expectancy.

Not to be morbid, but thinking about how long we may be around is important for determining our best claiming strategy. If you have a shorter life expectancy for whatever reason, it may make sense to claim at age 62. Another consideration is to think about how long folks in your family tend to live. If people in your family live to be 95, it may not be best to claim early. We also need to consider our health situation. We want to think about our lifestyle too. Do you participate in activities that may be harmful to your health and longevity? Or are you in superman shape because you live at the gym and only eat carrots? All these things play into our life expectancy. If you have a shorter life expectancy due to medical issues, then it might make sense to claim Social Security as soon as possible. However, if you're healthy and go to the doctor on a regular basis, you may want to consider what a long life will do to your finances. Tom Hegna, an author and economist, considers longevity to be a risk multiplier[8], because we have longer to plan for. Makes sense, right? This brings us to the elephant in the room.

According to a 2022 Go Banking Rates survey[9], "66% of Americans fear that they will run out of money during retirement. Additionally, 50% stated that they are concerned that they will have an unexpected major health expense, and 21% worry that they'll be forced to retire earlier than expected." That's a big number of people. Getting a plan together is essential, and that starts with figuring out your optimal Social Security claiming strategy for you and your spouse. Did you know that according to the 2020 census there were[10] 97,104 people living in America who were 100 or older?

What happens if you live to 100? Let's imagine you're 100 now and looking back over your retirement. You likely started thinking about retirement a half a century ago. How would you plan if you knew you'd live to be 100? While we know everyone won't live to be that old, it's a good thought exercise.

3

WHAT IS A SUSTAINABLE WITHDRAWAL RATE?

*I*t depends. A sustainable withdrawal rate is contingent on several factors. Let's get into them. When I started my financial services company in 2018, a lot depended on me. If you've ever started a business, you are acutely aware of what I mean. When you write all the checks, everything depends on you and the product of your work. Well, in retirement everything depends on you too, because you've entered the distribution phase of saving and investing. You're at a major crossroads and your retirement success may depend on a few decisions you make. Let's step back for a moment and I'll explain the two different types of investors.

When we are working and we have a long time horizon before retirement, we are in an "accumulation phase." We are trying to accumulate as much money as possible. If we're age 42 and 25 years from retirement and our equity positions take a 35% nosedive in one year, it probably doesn't matter. Why? Because we have the benefit of time. We have a long time horizon, and the stock market normally corrects and gains over time.

Nick Murray in the book *Simple Wealth, Inevitable Wealth*[1] states that the stock market goes up 70 to 75% of the time. It's the 25% that we have to look out for when we are in our distribution phase. When we are within five years of retirement or we are in retirement, we may want to transition into an "income and distribution phase," with the goal being to develop a plan for how we can take distributions out of our financial portfolio and make our money last as long as possible.

We have a proverbial golden goose which is our portfolio of investments. Our golden goose lays golden eggs and we want to harvest the eggs. We don't want to harvest the goose! How do we keep from having to eat our golden goose?

In 1994, financial advisor Bill Bengen[2] came up with the "4% rule," and his research concluded that in retirement we should have 55% of our portfolio in large cap stocks and 45% of our portfolio in government Treasury bonds. We should begin withdrawing 4% per year in retirement and increase withdrawals for inflation each year. With this methodology, Bengen hypothesized that we have a pretty good likelihood of not running out of money in a 30-year retirement. This idea seems to have evolved into the 60/40 rule where 60% of a retiree's money is allocated to equities and 40% to bonds. You may have heard this referred to as the "balanced portfolio."

In 1994[3] the Treasury bond yield averaged 7.09% and got as high as 8.05%. Since then, Treasury yields have been much lower than 7 or 8% most of the time. It's been my observation in meeting with hundreds of retirees that Bengen's rule is broken. In a 2022 Wall Street Journal[4] article, Bengen said, "The problem is that there's no precedent for today's [economic] conditions." And therein lies another problem.

Let's look at a a hypothetical* example of a couple just entering retirement and referred to our firm. The reason they were looking for another option was their advisor had $500,000 of their $1.7 million in underperforming bonds. They wanted a different strategy, but their financial advisor wasn't using all the tools available to help reach their goals for retirement. That left them wanting. They wanted a plan in place to reach those goals. I don't blame them, because who wouldn't want all their money earning as much interest as possible? I know I do!

In 2022, the 60/40 portfolio experienced its worst decline since 2008[5]. The main culprit was that interest rates had a rapid ascent. The Federal Reserve raised rates to attempt to calm inflation levels that had not been seen in 40 years. Remember, bonds carry risk. When interest rates increase, bond values go down. What if there was a bond substitute that doesn't lose money based on stock market decline and was more protected than a bond? We'll get to that later.

Since the War on Terror began in the early 2000s, we've seen record national deficits and in recent years, highly contentious legislatures. The latter means little monetary change happens because of the lack of consensus. So, what is a retiree to do with the prospect that Social Security may get cut, they could face uninsured medical costs in retirement, and the government is trillions of dollars in debt?

If you say run and hide or put your head in the sand, you may find a lot of company. It's easy to want to curl up in a ball and hope it all goes away, but it won't. Innately, as humans we need to hope that things will be better. To that end, our goal is to help our clients have as much confidence in retirement as possible. That's what we strive for every day. It's our goal with every interaction. It's satisfying when one of our clients states they feel better about their retirement outlook after we've implemented their customized financial plan. Having clients express their deep-felt gratitude for our help, that's worth more than money to us. Hearing we helped people have a more confident retirement is why we exist as a firm.

The scenarios shown herein are for illustrative purposes only and are based on hypothetical assumptions. These are not actual clients of the financial professional or firm.

4
HOW TIMES ARE CHANGING

Baby Boomers have the benefit of having lived through the post-World War II economic boom and the strong bull markets of the 1990s and the 2010s. They are familiar with prosperous economic times and may believe America always finds a way. This often creates optimism about the future. I've observed that Baby Boomers often have the mentality that America will figure it out, because we always have. Recently, Russia arrested a Wall Street Journal reporter named Evan Gershkovich on espionage charges. The Journal interviewed[1] his parents who had immigrated from Russia many years ago. When Evan's mom was asked if she still has hope that her son will be released, she said they had adopted the American mentality that a brighter future is coming. Basically, it's the American way to hope for things to be resolved and problems to work themselves out.

Recently, I was meeting with some prospective clients, and I always ask a question the first time I sit down with people. I ask, "How are you feeling about the stock market?" The answers are revealing, and naturally they're different depending on if we are in a bull or bear market. When I asked this couple my standard question, the stock market had been in a slump for a while. I got a similar response about the stock market feeling pretty lousy right now, but they believed it would come back. Up until that time, I normally would just nod and write my notes about their response.

I love reading books and listening to podcasts. The late Zig Ziglar [2] used to say that if you live in an average metropolitan area, you can learn in three years of driving time what you can learn in two years at a university. I took that advice literally a few years back and started "redeeming my time" as Paul wrote about in Ephesians.

I had listened to a Tony Robbins podcast a few weeks before I met with the couple in my office, and Robbins brought an interesting point to light. Robbins discussed with his podcast guest how some Millennials are aging into their early 40s now, and those individuals are beginning to assume important executive-level roles in industry, in news organizations and across the economy. Millennials are gaining positions of influence. I'm a Millennial and as of this writing, I recently entered my 40s, so this piqued my interest. Robbins said this to illustrate that my generation has had a different set of experiences than Baby Boomers. I started voting around the time of the September 11th terrorist attacks. My generation has seen the government spend trillions of dollars on misguided, losing wars. And, we've seen politician after politician mismanage our national resources. The maleficence transcends party lines. It's only natural for people my age to have a different perspective than Baby Boomers, who had much different experiences.

I want to believe the future is going to be brighter than the past. I invest in equities every month because I need to believe that what's to come will be better, but I believe it's prudent to remember the lenses through which we are seeing our circumstances may be different from another person or our perspective may be different from actual reality. Sometimes it's hard to realize our own blind spots. Now that I've thrown a wet blanket on the situation, let's move on!

So, how do we figure out what a sustainable withdrawal rate is? We figure out what our Social Security will be and how to best withdraw from Social Security to maximize our lifetime payout for us and our spouse. We determine if we have any defined benefit pensions or income sources. Then, we figure out what our income needs will be. In an ideal world we are going to attempt to project what we'll need for the next 10 years. Let's dive into the specifics.

5

THE THREE ROLES OF MONEY AND SPECIFICS ON INVESTMENTS

*L*et's talk about the *Three Roles of Money*. It's our proprietary system of illustrating how your funds should be invested as we get close to retirement or we are in retirement. We believe in keeping things simple in our office, so we color code the types of money. We have **green**, **blue**, and **red** money. When people visit with me in my office, I draw this out on a whiteboard. When I meet with prospective clients on Zoom, I'll draw it out on my iPad. I always preface it with a joke about not being an artist. In my office, I have artwork my wife has created. She could draw or create just about anything. Believe me. I've tested her! When you live with someone who's so talented, it keeps you keenly aware of your artistic inabilities, but maybe that's what marriage is for: to keep you humble.

Anyhow, our **green** money bucket is for money that's in the bank, and we use it for regular bill paying. We want to have six-to-nine months of bill-paying money in the bank. Then if we have an emergency, we hopefully don't need to use credit to pay for the emergency expense. And, we don't have to have a fire sale on our investments and possibly sell our holdings at an inopportune time. If we don't have an emergency fund, we may have to use a high-interest credit card. It can be hard to get credit cards paid down if we have to pay double-digit interest rates. If we have a fire sale on our investments, we may even incur taxes if we are liquidating retirement accounts. We want to avoid these things by having an emergency fund in our **green** bucket.

If we have more than one year of bill-paying in the bank, then generally speaking, we have lazy money. Do you know what lazy money is? It's funds that are not working for us and not earning enough interest. Typically, banks pay very little interest and normally when they do pay interest, it's treading water with the inflation level. In the years after the COVID-19 pandemic, inflation has been high. If inflation is 7% per year and we have $100,000 parked in the bank, how much purchasing power did we lose in one year? Our $100,000 now buys $93,000. That's a certain loss, and it is to our advantage to always avoid certain losses. We have to attempt to combat that and we need to try to keep up with inflation to protect our purchasing power. This means we don't want too much money in our **green** bucket.

Next, we have our **red** bucket. You probably already know what this is. It's our stock market money. We need money in the market throughout our lifetime. In our early years as we are working, we invest in the market to grow our nest egg to ultimately use in retirement or to bequeath to our beneficiaries.

Also, the stock market may protect our purchasing power, because the market tends to grow with the economy. Fortunately, the stock market often helps us maintain our purchasing power in retirement, so we need money allocated to the market at all points of life. What I mean by protecting our purchasing power is that the stock market tends to help ensure we will be able to buy the same goods in the future with the same investments that we have today. Historically, the stock market has been a hedge against inflation.

Our strategy with **red** bucket investments changes from year to year depending on what is going on in the market, politically, and on our client's risk tolerance. Our typical goal is to invest in equities that don't touch the top of a mountain graph, so we are not investing in companies that are expected to outperform the overall market. We shy away from trying to outperform the market because when we swing for home runs, we have to be willing to strike out too. In other words, we have to be okay with experiencing the lowest lows of the market. If we can find equities that can earn a moderate return on average, we hopefully won't have to experience the worst of the market drops, but we won't experience the highest highs of the stock market either.

To continue the baseball analogy, in retirement we are looking for ground balls. Remember, in retirement it's important to be in an income and distribution stance. We were in an accumulation stance when we had a long time horizon before we needed to use our money. Making a transition with our finances is necessary when retirement is on the horizon or we are in retirement. We have to balance this with our need to have growth though, so that we can protect our purchasing power. Plus, some people may live thirty years in retirement which necessitates having growth in our accounts. Our goal is to build all-weather financial plans so that we can benefit in good markets, but we don't perish in bad markets. We put guardrails on accounts so we don't go over a cliff when things outside of our control happen in the economy and stock market.

You may have heard a common retort when someone is expressing their concern about not taking on too much risk. It normally goes like this: "The stock market will always come back. You haven't lost anything until you sell and you lock in your losses." Or, "You just experienced paper losses. Just hang on."

Recently, I had a client in the office who had recently transitioned his accounts to us. He transitioned to us because he liked that we were focused on downside protection. He had recently attended a seminar and the financial advisor said a couple of the above lines. It didn't sit well with this client. As he sat there at the seminar, he looked around and saw people who had worked many years to save for retirement and use their funds to create a retirement that they had always wanted. If he had to potentially wait for years for his funds to recover from an unruly stock market, he may run out of years to enjoy the retirement he spent years planning and aspire to lead.

We have to be balanced in our approach and use various financial and insurance vehicles so that we can create as much protection as possible for ourselves. Unfortunately, this client didn't feel that his current advisor was using all the tools to help reach his financial and retirement goals. We'll talk more about that in a few pages. Also, please remember we need funds in the market, but we should be judicious with how go about it.

Warren Buffett is the famous guy[1] who may be the greatest stock market investor who's lived. In his 1996 shareholder letter[2] he wrote, "Put together a portfolio of companies whose aggregate earnings march upward over the years, and so also will the portfolio's market value. If you aren't willing to own a stock for 10 years, don't even think about owning it for 10 minutes."

Put another way, Buffett said[3], "Nobody buys a farm based on whether they think it's going to rain next year. They buy it because they think it's a good investment over 10 or 20 years." But this begs the question, if I'm holding equities for 10 years, how do I create retirement income? Wall Street may lead you to believe you should just sell a sliver of your equities every month to create your "mailbox money," but this violates Buffett's 10-year rule. The other option is leaving a couple years of income money in cash, but is that the best use of our funds? After all, we're losing purchasing power each year we are not invested.

What we do in our office is section off our **green** money and **blue** money from our **red** bucket. To figure out what we need to put in the **blue** bucket, we should calculate what we project our expenses will be for the next 10 years. Remember when we talked about figuring out what it takes to crack your nut each month? We add in any other expected expenses like the purchase of a vehicle, vacations, medical expenses, or taxes or whatever the case may be. We put that in the **blue** bucket. Some people find this challenging to figure out. If that's you, then we generally recommend putting 40% to 60% in the **blue** bucket. But, you would likely benefit from figuring out a more precise amount of money to allocate to the **blue** bucket.

What we are looking for as far as asset allocation in the **blue** bucket is something that will generate a bond-like return with as little variance as possible. It has to earn interest so that our money is not lazy. That rules out most bank products. The idea is to draw the **blue** bucket down over 10 years. Then, we are letting our **red** bucket run.

Let's face it. We're all emotional creatures. It's human nature. If we have 100 percent of our money in the **red** stock market bucket and we turn on the TV or go to our favorite news apps on our smartphone and we see the stock market is plunging, what is our gut reaction? Panic! We may not panic too much if we are 10, 15, or 25 years from retirement, but imagine retiring next year and the market crashes this year. I think it's safe to assume most people would be worried.

We know the stock market is up more days than it is down and it's a wealth generator. But sometimes our instincts are to want to sell our positions at the bottom of the market or when it's falling. That may be the worst possible time to sell! What if you had a strategy for times like these? What if you had 10 years of income in the **blue** bucket that was stabilized and not nose-diving when the stock market corrects? You may be able to turn the TV off and forget it because normally the market will come back within 10 years.

You have time for your money to recover. The idea here is to allocate our long-term growth money to the market and let it ride after we have our income money segregated out. This allows us the benefit of time if our **red** bucket money experiences a downturn. The goal here is to never have to sell our equity positions in a down market, because we know if we sell in a down market then mathematically our money does not last as long as if we had sold our positions in a level or appreciated position.

The next step is to plug a few numbers into a financial calculator to figure out what you can sustainably draw out of your account without running out of money before we run out of life. Then we'll draw down the **blue** bucket over the next 10 years. This allows the **red** bucket to run, and it combats our human tendency to sell out of the stock market at bad times.

When we're going through this exercise on the whiteboard in our office, sometimes astute people will ask what to invest the **blue** bucket in. There are three main categories of assets we can use for the **blue** bucket. We can use bonds. We talked about some of the problems with bonds in Chapter 4. Up until the year 2022, bonds have not been paying that well for a long time. We saw interest rates swiftly rise in the years after the COVID-19 pandemic. Prior to this, bonds yields had been paying very little.

In 2022[4], the S&P 500 lost 19.4% of its value. In the same year, Santa Clara University professor Edward McQuarrie declared it the worst year on record for bond investors. The Federal Reserve had rapidly increased interest rates to their highest levels since the high-rate period of the early 1980s. This was done to try to offset record-high inflation. Generally speaking, the government has been sitting on the side of the table of investors, and the Federal Reserve and government entities have attempted to keep the stock market up and the economy growing. The government has done this by keeping interest rates ultra-low to make it easier for folks to buy homes, finance vehicles, and borrow money.

It used to be cheap to borrow money. This helped keep the demand high for products and helped keep people in jobs because there was demand for new widgets. During the COVID-19 pandemic, the government created new money. One of the things the government decided to do was to send what the IRS calls "economic impact payments," or stimulus checks, when the economy was shut down during the COVID-19 scare. By infiltrating the economy with new money, it devalued our money and we lost purchasing power. This is inflation. This is in large part what caused the Total Bond Index[5] to lose 13% in 2022. When interest rates rise, bond values go down.

Remember the couple who was referred to me with $1.7 million saved for retirement and their advisor has them in a 60/40 split of equities and bonds? The reason they were referred to me is because they were irritated that their bonds were not earning much interest. They wanted a different strategy. So, what else can we use besides bonds?

Some people prefer to use dividend-paying stocks to generate income. There are no guarantees that dividends will always be paid. While they may be somewhat predictable, any time we are using equities, we do not have guarantees, protection or certainty. The value of a dividend paying-stock may go down in value thereby washing out the dividend.

What I've observed is normally if a person is working with a financial advisor, they are using whatever their advisor is allowed to use under his agreement with his or her employer. Whose interest is being preserved in that scenario? We'll talk more about how to pick a financial advisor in a few pages.

The third asset class we can use in the **blue** bucket is an annuity. While some annuities are good, there are also annuities that may not be great for your income situation. Tread carefully here. It's important in any annuity conversation to understand what type of annuity is being discussed. I've observed that sometimes people will mix details of the different types of annuities up, and it creates misinformation. Let's run through the different kinds.

Fixed annuities have been around in America for over a 100 years. They pay a set interest rate for a set number of years. They have a defined outcome. We know exactly what we are going to get when we put money in a fixed annuity. They work a lot like a certificate of deposit, or CD, does from a bank. The difference is that annuities are issued from insurance companies, and it's been my experience that they normally pay a little more than a CD. There is no way to lose money due to market risks.

The next kind of annuity came out in 1995, and they are fixed indexed annuities. With this type, we are participating with the growth of the stock market or an index, but we are not "in" the stock market or index. Therefore, we can't lose any of our initial premium. This type of account uses the stock market or the index as a bellwether or gauge for how the market has done and credits interest accordingly. With this type of annuity, you are not directly invested in the stock market.

I would say there are two main types of fixed indexed annuities. There are ones that are geared for safe accumulation and there are ones that are geared for guaranteed income. If you are looking for a stable place to grow your funds with no downside risk, then an accumulation-style indexed annuity may work for you.

When interest rates are ultra-low or near-zero percent, this type of annuity is designed to earn what a bond should be earning. These can have uncapped indexing strategies so you may earn a double-digit return from time to time, and some years you may earn nothing. A properly designed accumulation-style annuity can earn what a typical bond would earn with less risk. Often, they have no management fees either. If interest rates are elevated, you may expect to earn more, because annuities are highly favored when interest rates rise. Why?

When an insurance company issues an annuity, they may invest a portion of the money in long-term bonds. With a smaller portion of the money deposited, they may use an options strategy as a hedge. When an insurance company can earn more on their money, they may pay their clients more.

All annuities are set up on a declining surrender charge schedule which means they ask that a depositor leave their money invested for a period of time. With fixed annuities, the time period ranges from two years to 10 years. With indexed annuities it's typically five, seven, or 10 years. This is not an arbitrary thing where the insurance company says, "Yes, we've got David for 10 years!" No, what is happening is the actuaries at insurance companies have figured out that if they can work with our money for a period of time then they can make money on our money. The insurance company invests our funds on their books. They assume the risk. We do not have risk of loss with fixed annuities. The surrender charge allows the insurance company to recover any losses they may incur for unwinding their positions.

Generally, the longer we leave our money with the insurance company, the higher the interest we earn. With a many of the indexed annuities available, the annuity owner will be able to withdraw up to 10% of their money per year after the first contract year. If the annuity owner needs more than 10% in any year, they would incur a penalty. The penalty goes down as the account gets closer to maturation. This is why it's never suitable to put all of a person's money into an annuity. We find that the most suitable approach is not to put more than 60% of our investable assets in an annuity. An annuity can be a great tool in comprehensive financial planning, but it should not be the only financial product we are using. We need some market exposure to protect our purchasing power.

The other type of fixed indexed annuity is one that is geared for guaranteed income. Some people really like the sound of the word "guaranteed." With this type of annuity, you have the main chassis that's participating in the growth of the stock market but not in it, and then you have a separate value that grows at a specified rate no matter what. It does not matter if the stock market completely comes off the rails, because the income value (the separate value from the main chassis) is going to grow. The separate value is designed for one function, and that is to create a guaranteed stream of income for the rest of your life.

Think about Social Security. Let's say based on your work history that the government is going to pay you $2,000 per month in Social Security benefits. You have $24,000 rolling in every year as long as you wake up in the morning. If you pass away prematurely, there's no recourse. You helped all the other Social Security recipients in the pool. The $24,000 is what we call your income floor. If you spent the rest of your retirement funds or lost them, you know you still have $24,000 coming in every year.

Well, with a guaranteed income annuity you could increase your income floor. Let's say you could get another $2,000 per month guaranteed to be deposited into your bank account each month. You've increased your income floor up to $48,000 per year. The difference between this annuity and Social Security is that if you pass away prematurely, whatever money is left in the annuity is going to go to your beneficiaries. The insurance company does not get to keep any of your money.

On the flip side, if you live a really long life and all of your money is depleted out of the annuity, the insurance is contractually obligated to continue paying you as long as you are alive. It's longevity protection. This is *not* annuitization. If there is value left in the annuity when the holder of the annuity passes away, the balance will be paid to their beneficiary. The insurance company does not get to keep the balance in the account.

The idea with an income-orientated fixed indexed annuity is to defer it a few years and allow it to earn its guaranteed interest, then turn it on. You normally can turn on the income after one year. Now, let's talk about some of the negatives to accumulation and income fixed indexed annuities.

With an income annuity it's only a good deal if you are relatively certain you're going to turn the guaranteed income portion on at some point in the future. Why? Well, you will often have a fee that you pay for the income feature (currently around 1 to 1.35%). So, if nothing else, you've paid for something you're not using. Secondly, when we buy an income annuity, we normally don't earn as much as an accumulation annuity earns. We may experience reduced earnings on the main chassis of the account. So, if we did not turn the income on, we have diminished our long-term returns.

With an accumulation-style annuity, we are guaranteed to not lose any of our initial premium. This is also the case for income annuities but with an accumulation-style, we are not guaranteed a return either. We are able to earn up to 30-40% of the S&P 500 returns with no downside risk. And for the ones we use in our office, they have no fees. We can take 10% of the value off per year for income. The great thing about these is if we don't want income, we don't have to take it. With an income-style annuity, some do not allow you to stop income once you start it.

The next kind of annuity is a variable annuity. They've been around for years, but they can't make up their mind what they want to be. Are they stock? Are they an annuity? They try to be a hybrid of both, but it's my opinion that they often don't fit into our financial plans. Why? Fees. All variable annuities have a mortality expense ratio. According to Investopedia[6] the mortality expense charge is on average 1.25% per year, but it could go as high as 1.70%. "It compensates the insurer for any losses that it might suffer as a result of unexpected events, including the death of the annuity holder."

Then variable annuities have subunits which is how the account is invested in the market. You may invest it conservatively, moderately or aggressively. A third-party money manager normally manages those accounts, and the manager has a family to feed too. So, expect another fee for the subunits. I've observed that often there may be various riders that do different things and they come with a fee too. Expect to pay several internal fees with variable annuities. And remember, you have to pay the fees before you make a return. I believe there are more efficient ways to get the good elements of annuities with indexed annuities and there are more efficient ways to get the good elements of the stock market with mutual funds and ETFs. So, we steer clear of variable annuities.

It's important to understand the different types of annuities if you're ever researching them because if we mix details of the different types up, what do you think it would produce? If you said something nobody would want, you're right. When we mix up the details, it causes misinformation. Like anything, it's important to define the terms of the discussion.

6

TAXES AND USING ROTH IRAS

Nobody likes to talk about it, but we all know it's inevitable. Taxes! Let's talk about why a tax plan is necessary in retirement. If you're like many of the people who come into our office, you've used a 401(k) or a tax-deferred retirement plan to save for retirement. There's nothing inherently wrong with that, but it's important to understand that when we take our money out in retirement, we'll pay our ordinary income tax rate at whatever the tax rate is at that time. If you have a million dollars saved up and you're in a 25% tax bracket you really only have $750,000, right?

Tax-deferred accounts are helpful when we're working because they lower our taxable income and the IRS allows us to keep our tax money for compounding purposes. So, our money is able to grow more quickly. The problem is we don't know what our tax rate will be when we're retired. Many people have come to believe that they'll be in a lower tax bracket in retirement, and that may have been the way qualified retirement accounts were sold when they originated in the 1970s. But it's important to understand that back then, Social Security was not taxed and today retirees often pay tax on their Social Security benefits. Also, remember that distributions from retirement accounts are taxed as ordinary income or like your regular paycheck while you are working.

The other challenge is the U.S. has not had a balanced budget since 2001[1], and currently we are over $34 trillion in debt with no reduction in sight. It's plausible that taxes may need to increase to compensate for our high debt burden. Remember that the only way the government generates revenue is from taxpayers like you and me. What happens to your tax-deferred account when a government funding crisis erupts? More of your or your family's hard-earned dollars may be taxed. Wouldn't it be good if you could immunize your accounts against future taxation?

You're in luck! We can help you transition tax-deferred accounts to tax-free accounts. We can create a plan to pay some of your taxes today while tax rates are low and place the money in Roth IRA accounts. Then, the money plus any gains will never be taxed again. And, if you pass away with money still in your account, then it generally will pass tax-free to your beneficiaries. What we don't want to do is to take your whole balance out and transition it to tax-free in one year. You may increase your taxes to the highest level possible by doing that, which is not what we want to do. We want to stage our tax-paying out over several years to not increase our tax rate unnecessarily.

We work closely with accountants when we assist our clients in setting up an efficient tax strategy. We review the clients' tax returns for a couple years. Then, we lean heavily on accountant partners to provide insights on what the best methodology will be for transitioning funds from tax-deferred to tax-free accounts.

Paying taxes in advance is always a tough pill to swallow, but if you believe taxes will be higher in your lifetime, it may be important to consider the tax implications of your accounts. Also, if you're legacy minded and want to leave money to your children, and you believe taxes will be higher during your child's life, that may be an important consideration too.

I am certainly not advocating for *not* paying taxes. I believe we should pay what we owe, but our system allows us to structure our affairs in such a way that we may pay less in taxes. A famous judge named Learned Hand said in 1947,[2] "Any one may so arrange his affairs that his taxes shall be as low as possible; he is not bound to choose that pattern which will best pay the Treasury; there is not even a patriotic duty to increase one's taxes."

When tax-deferred accounts originated over 40 years ago, the idea was many people will be in a lower tax bracket when they retire, so you'll pay less taxes on tax-deferred money when you withdraw it to supplement Social Security and any pensions we may have. The challenge is that's not always the case. One culprit may be Social Security taxation. Prior to the 1980s, Social Security was not taxable at the federal level. As we mentioned earlier, Social Security's solvency issue is nothing new, so in 1983 President Reagan, a Republican, got together with Democrat Speaker of the House Tip O'Neill to forge a plan to tax Social Security[3] and increase the full retirement age[4] from 65 to 67, which as of this writing, is still being phased in today. Here's how it works.

The legislation coined a new term which is "provisional income," and it's all of your income plus half of your Social Security income. This includes[5] tax-free municipal bond interest, wages, distributions from 401(k)s and IRAs, interest and dividend income, capital gains, pension payments, and taxable portions of inheritance. Just about all types of income are included. What's not included is tax-free Roth IRA money. This may be another strong case for doing Roth conversions, because having money in a tax-free position may allow you to keep more of your Social Security.

If you file your taxes as single and you earn under $25,000, then none of your Social Security is taxable. If you make between $25,000 and $34,000, then up to 85% of your Social Security is taxable. If you file as single and you make over $34,000, then up to 85% of your benefits are taxable.

Now for married couples the thresholds are slightly higher. If you make less than $32,000, then none of your Social Security benefits are taxable. If you make between $32,000 and $44,000, then up to 50% of your benefits are taxable. If you make over $44,000 then up to 85% of your benefits are taxable.

We do a lot of Social Security workshops in our community, because aging into Social Security and Medicare can be overwhelming for people to figure out on their own. I have a slide with the above numbers stated. I always pause after reviewing and ask, "What are your thoughts after seeing this?" Just about everyone is going to pay some taxes on their Social Security. These numbers have not changed since the 1980s.

In 1983, one dollar was equivalent to about $3.02 today. Meaning it takes more money to buy the same goods as it did then. Remember when we said we need money allocated to our **red** stock market bucket throughout our lifetimes? This is why, because the market may help us combat rising prices.

Fortunately, only 11 states tax [6]our Social Security benefits. But the point remains that because of the changes to our tax system, often we find people pay a similar rate of taxes in retirement as they do while working.

7

WHAT ELSE CAN WE DO TO SAVE ON TAXES?

We're just getting started after we have our Roth conversion plan figured out. Let's talk about the 7702 accounts. That's the IRS code for this type of account and how it stays tax-free. It's a type of life insurance we buy at reduced cash value so that we can max fund the policy for its tax-free benefits. We typically aren't buying life insurance for the death benefit only. We are buying it for the living benefits as well.

The government allows us to fund these over five years, or technically speaking four years and one day. But why may we do this? We go ahead and pay the taxes on the money we put into the 7702 accounts and over five years it builds a cash value. Normally in a few years, we can get hold of those tax-free dollars. This type of account takes some time to marinate and keep up and running. This is a secondary strategy after we have begun or completed Roth conversions. There are different types of 7702 accounts, but the emphasis should be on using an account that is not in the stock market.

If we take our funds out properly, they will be tax-free. Where this shines even more as a possibly viable vehicle to use is if we don't think we'll need the funds we are putting in the plan in our lifetime because the death benefit will typically blossom into a larger tax-free benefit for the beneficiaries.

8

WHAT TO DO WHEN THE STOCK MARKET IS DOWN

*D*own markets open up opportunities for tax efficiency planning. In January 2020, the market was trading at all-time highs and the economy was doing well, but come February everything changed. The COVID-19 pandemic began in haste and the market began selling off due to fear of the unknown. The S&P 500 was down well over 30% that year[1]. We may be able to take advantage of a black swan event like COVID-19. When a stock is at a low in our taxable account, we can sell the asset and book a loss on paper. Then, we can buy back a similar but different stock or wait at least 31 days to buy the same stock. But remember, with the COVID-19 correction the rebound happened quickly. We may not want to wait a month. This strategy allowed us to offset up to $3,000 of ordinary income taxes that year, and we could carry forward losses over $3,000. This is called tax loss harvesting.[2]

9
LET'S TALK ABOUT QCDS

*A*re you over age 69? Do you donate to charity? If you answered yes to both questions, this strategy may be for you. You technically need to be age 70.5 years according to the IRS to make qualified charitable distributions (QCD) from your IRA, but pre-planning is helpful. Remember, you can't make these from a 401(k). If you have a 401(k) and want to make a QCD, you must roll your funds over to an IRA.

You can give up to $100,000 per person to a charity of your choice. If you're taking required minimum distributions (RMDs), you may want to think about this strategy. If you give funds to your church, a school, or charity on a consistent basis, this strategy may allow you to give even more than you realized is possible.

If you take funds out of your IRA and then cut a check to your church, you pay taxes on the distribution. A QCD allows you to send the funds directly from the custodian holding your funds to a 501c3, bypassing paying taxes on the funds as the church receives more money. We give money to organizations we are passionate about. Why not try to stretch those funds?

10

HERE'S ANOTHER TAX EFFICIENCY STRATEGY

A donor-advised fund may allow for tax advantages also. The donor donates cash or assets to the fund and then the donor will ask the fund to make distributions to the charity. The donor gets the tax deduction the year they make the donation. Our funds have to go into a foundation that manages the fund, administers the process, and ensures it is IRS compliant.

Let's say we have a couple taking the standard deduction and not itemized deductions on taxes. We could give a few years of donations to the donor-advised fund so we can take advantage of the tax deduction. Then, the funds are invested based on the client's risk tolerance. We generally want to invest the funds conservatively because the idea is to donate the funds in the next few years. But at any rate, say you put $45,000, or three years of contributions, into the fund. Then, the investment will hopefully grow and thereby allow us to donate even more than we originally put in the fund.

We get to put the original donation on Schedule A, which currently is larger than the standard deduction. This allows us to save on our taxes. Everyone's situation may be a little different. We may be able to use this tax savings to pay the taxes on our Roth conversions we talked about in the first strategy.

Let's say you have a portfolio of individual stocks. We can donate our highly appreciated stock into the donor-advised fund. We can sell it the next day and write ourselves a check and buy the same stock back and avoid paying the capital gains on the position. Then, when we need to sell for a liquidity event, we potentially don't have as much tax liability.

11

LET'S TALK ABOUT RECENT LEGISLATIVE CHANGES

*P*rior to 2020, if we obtained the age of 70.5 and had a qualified retirement plan like an IRA, 401(k), or 403b, the IRS mandated we begin taking a required minimum distribution (RMD). You are no longer able to defer paying the taxes on your funds. Legislation called the SECURE Act increased the age to 72. Then in 2023, the SECURE Act 2.0 created a phased-in process that works like this: If we are born between 1951 and 1959, we must begin taking our RMDs at age 73. For folks born in 1960 or after, the age to begin is 75.

This legislation was celebrated by many people, but is there more to it than what meets the eye? Perhaps. By delaying the taxes another year and a half or to four and half years longer, our funds will generally grow during that deferral period. Who do you think benefits? If you said Uncle Sam, you'd be correct. You may end up paying more on those funds.

Also, the calculation used to determine what amount we are to take out of our accounts is based on our mortality. The older we are, the shorter our life expectancy is. What's worse is we hear statistics about life expectancy increasing, but it has actually been decreasing lately. This may be in part because of illicit drugs, obesity, the Fentanyl crisis, and COVID. Obviously, some of these things are lifestyle choices which may not impact us if we take care of ourselves. So, the likely scenario is you live longer but have to take out more funds more quickly due to the shorter life expectancy tables. Plus, when we defer taxes on our qualified accounts, we are taking the chance of paying more in taxes if rates go up. This may be a compelling reason to consider the tax efficiency strategies we've outlined here.

These are a few of the things to be aware of when it comes to taxes in retirement. Next, let's talk about how to go about getting advice.

12

HOW TO PICK A FINANCIAL ADVISOR

      There's more than one way to go about many things, but I'm sure you understand your author has his preferences on the best ways to go about finding your ideal financial planner. Let's start with the evolution of advice in financial services.

    Back in the days before the Internet, if you wanted to buy stock or bonds you needed a broker. The stockbroker normally made a commission for selling stocks to their customers. It was more of a transactional relationship. It was kind of like going to your favorite department store to buy clothes. You browse through the racks of clothes and when you pick out what you want, you take them to the register to buy. In some stores, the clerk may suggest certain clothes based on what you need the clothes for and help you pick out a shirt or a pair of pants. When it came to buying stocks or bonds, the investor needed to know there were limitations on how they could trade in the stock market, and they needed a liaison to facilitate buying equities.

    Fast forward to the Internet age and things slowly started to improve for consumers. When people could place trades themselves from the comfort of their home, a stockbroker was no longer needed to get access to the stock market. One benefit the broker may have been providing was some level of advice regarding which stocks to allocate to when placing trades. But with the Internet came a plethora of advice columns and the rise of "do it yourself" (DIY) investing.

I speak with many people each year who have successfully become their own financial advisor and accumulated a substantial degree of assets. The challenge DIY investors have is that accumulating assets isn't always difficult, especially when the federal government is accommodative to the stock market. For example, when interest rates are ultra-low like they have been for much of the 21st century, the stock market tends to do very well, but if you happen to hit your retirement age at a challenging economic time, then things may get dicey. Figuring out the best path forward may become challenging.

If you entered retirement around the year 2000, you would have had wildly different circumstances than if you entered retirement in 2010. I'd say most people who come to see us at our office have saved for 30 years, and in some cases 50 years, for retirement. Now they want to figure out the best way to begin utilizing their retirement savings. They are looking for an income and distribution plan. Or they just want to know they'll be okay if they retire.

That's what we do. We specialize in helping our clients put together financial plans that are focused on the decumulation phases of retirement. Knowing how you can spend your savings and make it last as long as possible is empowering. Back to our different outcomes.

In 2000, 2001, and 2002, the S&P 500 index had negative performance as it lost on average 15.5% each year. Then in 2008, the mortgage bubble exploded and the same index lost 38.5% that year. If you were in the market during this decade, you may have experienced a negative overall return and this time period is often referred to as the "lost decade[1]."

On the other hand, let's say you entered retirement in 2010. Then you would have been much better in terms of market returns. During the 2010s, the S&P 500 index of the stock market had one year, 2018, when it lost. It was down -4.23%.[2] Otherwise, the index was positive. In the first scenario if you were drawing money out of your accounts, you may have been left in a dire situation. In the latter scenario, you may have left the decade with more money than you started with and been able to withdraw a modest amount to supplement your Social Security income. This is called sequence of returns risk. The order in which you experience market fluctuations matters in retirement. When we are 10 or 20 years from retirement, it may not matter if your 401(k) sees a 30% decrease because we have the benefit of a long time horizon. If we're within five years of retirement or early on in retirement, stock market gyrations matter. There are steps you can take to mitigate this risk.

Becoming your own financial advisor is necessary for many people who have qualified retirement plans like the 401(k) which came out in 1978. Previously, many employers offered pension programs to their employees. My grandfather worked for a telephone company his whole career in the town where I grew up, and he knew when he went to work there as a young man that if he worked a certain number of years and if he made a certain amount of money when he retired, he'd have a certain amount of money in the form a pension payment for the rest of his life. Talk about retirement protection! A pension manager managed a defined benefit pension plan, and the manager would look at a hundred-year swath of time. The manager could predict boom and bust cycles in the economy with relative accuracy because human nature and other factors are somewhat predictable.

It reminds me of an Andy Griffith episode. A law student comes down to Mayberry to essentially intern with Andy and Barney to see how police operations work in real life. Of course, Barney's pride is hurt as he thinks there is a conspiracy to replace him and complains about it to Thelma Lou. One of the techniques the law student had learned was how to predict crime cycles, so he made a graphic on a board to demonstrate. And sure enough, he accurately predicted that there would be a wife beating.

In normal circumstances, a pension manager has training to be able to predict market cycles, but with the creation of the Federal Reserve in 1913 under President Woodrow Wilson, the government began attempting to periodically stimulate the economy for what we'll conclude are altruistic reasons.

The point is that when a third party got involved in the outcome of the economy and the free market no longer could dictate what happens in the economy, it became challenging for a pension manager to reliably predict boom and bust cycles in the economy.

So, the thinking began that perhaps the best thing to do would be to allow workers to become their own pension manager/financial planner, and then we had the introduction of the 401(k). This took the onus off employers, but it placed the financial burden on employees. This increased the risk of poor outcomes for the worker, and the responsibility of managing financial outcomes for retirees was no longer the employer's obligation.

When we are younger and we have a long time horizon before we'll need to access our funds, it may make sense to put our retirement savings in an index fund and let it ride. Sure, we'll have volatility, but in the long term we know historically we've had amazing growth. When we are within five years of retirement or we're in retirement, it makes sense to transition from an accumulation stance to an income and distribution stance. How are we going to create income from our funds we've been saving for 30 or more years? A good financial planner will be able to plot out a plan to make this work.

Our world is set up by specialties. When I have a nail in my tire, I go to the tire shop. I don't go to the mechanic who specializes in radiators. When I have a foot ache I don't go to the neurologist, I go to the podiatrist. Sure, there are family doctors who will see us for just about any medical reason, but they're normally quick to refer us to a specialist if our issue can't be quickly resolved in their office. I encourage you to find a financial advisor who specializes in helping folks retire or folks who are in retirement. Many firms work with folks who are setting up a 529 college savings plan for their newborn, or help 45-year-olds with IRA contributions, and they dabble across the spectrum. I've found it's best to go an inch wide and a mile deep so that I can become a master of my craft.

13

THE VALUE OF INDEPENDENCE

When we are talking about sensitive topics like our life savings, we want the most objective advice we can get, right? How can we get unbiased information from someone who works at a captive financial institution? Think about it this way. When I worked at Starbucks in college, when you entered our stores, you were there to buy a cup of Starbucks coffee. You weren't going to get Dunkin Donuts coffee. We understand this when it comes to tangible things we buy, but we sometimes forget that when we walk into a corporate-branded financial advisory firm. When someone complained to me at Starbucks that our coffee was bitter, I could add water, flavor or put whipped cream on top. But at the end of the day, it was still Starbucks coffee. We were going down the proverbial cattle chute one way or another. When you work with an independent advisor, you don't have to go down just one path. The advisor typically has taken on the risk of owning a business so that he or she can provide the most comprehensive selection of choices. That way we are not forced down one path for all our clients. This helps to eliminate conflicts of interest that a captive advisor may have. Also, it's not just about investment management. It's about caring for the whole person's financial wellbeing.

Obviously, there are good people who work at wire house firms or for the branded financial advisory offices you see everywhere, and good people may disagree with me. We are all a product of the environment we came up in, and I was fortunate enough to learn how to set up an independent financial advisory practice. And, the philosophy was pounded into me. I think working with an independent advisor is the best way to get the most holistic, comprehensive assistance.

14
CONCLUSION

Thanks for sticking with me on this journey. These ideas are a snapshot into how we help our clients create more satisfaction. Our mission is to help good people make wise financial decisions so that they may excel in retirement with confidence. We work with clients in various parts of the United States.

Obviously, we'd be happy to sit down with you and your spouse in person or by Zoom. Our *Excel in Retirement* process for how we help people works like this: We have a get-to-know-you discovery meeting where we learn about you and you learn about us and our firm. In our first interaction, we work through Social Security planning, your current income plan, your investment plan, income plan tax efficiency plan, healthcare plan, and legacy plan. If you don't have all of these things addressed in your plan, please consider the fact that you may not be getting all the value you could be. And unfortunately, there may be pitfalls that stand between you and a successful retirement.

We will talk about what you like about your situation. We look for ways to potentially optimize anything you may be doing. If we can identify ways we think we may be able to help you, we will invite you to come back in or schedule another Zoom call where we expand on our *Three Roles of Money* process we shared with you in our first strategy session. We will then present our analysis of your situation which outlines ways to improve what you're currently doing if there are any.

Our only "ask" from the session is for you to think about it and discuss it with your spouse. If we're still tracking together at the end of our second session, we'll invite you back for an implementation session. This is where we put the ball in motion and begin implementing the plan we have created for you. From there, we go to work behind the scenes ironing out all the details. Then, in about four to six weeks we reconvene and present your documents to you in a leather binder. We answer any questions you may have and schedule our next strategy session to update your plan in the next year. We want to stay in touch and have an ongoing relationship with our clients. Our goal is to have clients for life and we strive to offer second-to-none client service.

What you won't find with us is a high-pressure situation. We truly want what is best for our clients and those we interact with. We serve our clients with integrity and we treat each of the people we encounter with dignity, respect and honor. We value the trust our clients place in us to help them with their financial planning needs. We vow to never lose sight of always doing the right thing.

We would be honored to have an initial phone call with you to determine if sitting down together is appropriate at this time. We're not a good fit for everyone. But if you'd like to discover more about how we are different than many firms, please let us know. Also, I write a weekly newsletter that goes out on Wednesday mornings that has insights and updates in it. Visit my website to sign up for the newsletter. Here is my contact information:

David C. Treece, Financial Planner & Founder
Clients Excel
www.clientsexcel.com
hello@clientsexcel.com
864.641.7955

I wish you the best of success in your retirement planning journey! If you've found value in this guide, please share it with a friend.

ENDNOTES

1. DO YOU HAVE A PLAN?

1. "What Are 14ers," colorado.com, https://www.colorado.com/articles/what-are-14ers/
2. "Retirement Outlook 2024: Less Than Half Of Boomers Have Adequate Savings – Will Younger Generations Suffer?" https://www.nasdaq.com/articles/retirement-outlook-2024:-less-than-half-of-boomers-have-adequate-savings-will-younger#:~:text=Baby%20boomers%20haven't%20saved%20enough%20money%20for%20retirement&text=Forty%2Dthree%20percent%20of%2055,65%20are%20considered

2. SOCIAL SECURITY SIMPLIFIED: DETAILS AND WHAT TO LOOK OUT FOR

1. "Policy Basics," cbpp.org, https://www.cbpp.org/research/policy-basics-top-ten-facts-about-social-security
2. "Summary of the 2023 Annual Reports," ssa.gov https://www.ssa.gov/oact/trsum/
3. "Understanding the Benefits," ssa.gov, https://www.ssa.gov/pubs/EN-05-10024.pdf
4. "Details of Ida May Fuller's Payroll Tax Contributions," ssa.gov, https://www.ssa.gov/history/idapayroll.html
5. "Life expectancy," berkeley.edu, https://u.demog.berkeley.edu/~andrew/1918/figure2.html
6. "Delayed Retirement Credits," sss.gov https://www.ssa.gov/benefits/retirement/planner/delayret.html
7. "Retirement Charts," wsj.com, https://www.wsj.com/articles/retirement-charts-social-security-savings-health-efa1962b
8. "Why is longevity risk the #1 risk in retirement?," youtube.com, https://www.youtube.com/watch?v=Bmp4gwkDTac
9. "66% of Americans Are Worried They'll Run Out of Money in Retirement," nasdaq.com, https://www.nasdaq.com/articles/66-of-americans-are-worried-theyll-run-out-of-money-in-retirement-here-are-7-tips-to-make
10. "These Are the Nations With the Most People Over 100," usnews.com, https://www.usnews.com/news/best-countries/articles/2022-07-15/nations-with-the-most-people-over-100#:~:text=The%20United%20States%20came%20in,even%20better%20than%20the%20mainland.

ENDNOTES

3. WHAT IS A SUSTAINABLE WITHDRAWAL RATE?

1. Murray, Nick. "Simple Wealth, Inevitable Wealth: How You and Your Financial Advisor Can Grow Your Fortune in Stock Mutual Funds." New York, The Nick Murray Company, Inc, November 2000
2. "Cut Your Retirement Spending Now," wsj.com, https://www.wsj.com/articles/cut-your-retirement-spending-now-says-creator-of-the-4-rule-11650327097
3. "10 Year Treasury Rate", macrotrends.net, https://www.macrotrends.net/2016/10-year-treasury-bond-rate-yield-chart
4. "Cut Your Retirement Spending Now," wsj.com,https://www.wsj.com/articles/cut-your-retirement-spending-now-says-creator-of-the-4-rule-11650327097
5. "Inflation could make or break rebounding," finance.yahoo.com, https://finance.yahoo.com/news/inflation-could-break-rebounding-60-053319401.html

4. HOW TIMES ARE CHANGING

1. "Tense Wait for an Imprisoned Son," wsj.com, https://www.wsj.com/articles/a-tense-wait-for-an-imprisoned-son-9bf29415?mod=Searchresults_pos1&page=1
2. "Automobile University," youtube.com, https://www.youtube.com/watch?v=S1XZOXMXmAA

5. THE THREE ROLES OF MONEY AND SPECIFICS ON INVESTMENTS

1. "How Warren Buffett's winning investing strategy can be applied to any purchase you make," cnbc.com, https://www.cnbc.com/2018/05/04/warren-buffett-invests-for-the-long-term.html
2. "Chairman's Letter," berkshirehathaway.com, https://www.berkshirehathaway.com/letters/1996.html
3. "Warren Buffett's winning investing strategy," cnbc.com, https://www.cnbc.com/2018/05/04/warren-buffett-invests-for-the-long-term.html
4. "S&P 500," apnews.com, https://apnews.com/article/inflation-business-financial-markets-services-sydney-9c0001bbbffe827c85931b4d51908743
5. "2022 was the worst-ever year for U.S. bonds," cnbc.com, https://www.cnbc.com/2023/01/07/2022-was-the-worst-ever-year-for-us-bonds-how-to-position-for-2023.html#:~:text=Such%20long%2Ddated%20U.S.%20notes,bonds%20lost%2019%25%20in%201803.
6. "Mortality and Expense Risk Charge," investopedia.com, https://www.investopedia.com/terms/m/mortalityandexpenseriskcharge.asp

ENDNOTES

6. TAXES AND USING ROTH IRAS

1. "What is the national deficit?," fiscaldata.treasury.gov, https://fiscaldata.treasury.gov/americas-finance-guide/national-deficit/#:~:text=The%20U.S.%20has%20experienced%20a,the%20budget%20is%20considered%20balanced.
2. "Tax Avoidance Just Isn't What It Used To Be," forbes.com, https://www.forbes.com/sites/taxanalysts/2013/09/17/tax-avoidance-just-isnt-what-it-used-to-be/?sh=45c440685747
3. "Taxation of Social Security Benefits," ssa.gov, https://www.ssa.gov/history/taxationofbenefits.html
4. "Bipartisan Reagan-O'Neill Social Security Deal in 1983," usnews.com, https://www.usnews.com/opinion/articles/2009/04/02/bipartisan-reagan-oneill-social-security-deal-in-1983-showed-it-can-be-done
5. "How to Calculate Provisional Income," fool.com, https://www.fool.com/knowledge-center/how-to-calculate-provisional-income.aspx
6. "List of states that tax Social Security benefits," bankrate.com, https://www.bankrate.com/retirement/states-that-tax-social-security-benefits/#:~:text=For%20the%202022%20tax%20year,do%20not%20tax%20the%20payments.

8. WHAT TO DO WHEN THE STOCK MARKET IS DOWN

1. "The stock market is ending 2020 at record highs, even as the virus surges and millions go hungry," washingtonpost.com, https://www.washingtonpost.com/business/2020/12/31/stock-market-record-2020/
2. "Tax-Loss Harvesting," schwab.com, https://www.schwab.com/learn/story/how-to-cut-your-tax-bill-with-tax-loss-harvesting

12. HOW TO PICK A FINANCIAL ADVISOR

1. "The Lost Decade, Revisited," amgfunds.com, https://www.amgfunds.com/blog/the-lost-decade-revisited/#:~:text=The%20term%20%E2%80%9CLost%20Decade%20for,return%20over%20a%20decade%20period.
2. "S&P 500 Average Return and Historical Performance, Investopedia.com, https://www.investopedia.com/ask/answers/042415/what-average-annual-return-sp-500.asp

ABOUT THE AUTHOR
DAVID C. TREECE, FOUNDER OF CLIENTS EXCEL & FINANCIAL ADVISOR

David embarked on his journey in the financial services sector in 2011, initially serving as an assistant at two prominent firms before ascending to the role of financial advisor. Armed with a Series 65 securities exam certification and licensed in health and life insurance across Georgia, South Carolina, North Carolina, and Florida, David is committed to guiding his clients through the intricacies of retirement income and tax minimization planning.

In 2018, David laid the cornerstone of Clients Excel, driven by a vision to deliver unparalleled financial planning experiences to his clientele. His unwavering dedication stems from a profound desire to help equip individuals with the tools and strategies necessary to navigate retirement successfully, sidestepping potential pitfalls along the way.

At the heart of David's philosophy lies a steadfast commitment to the golden rule: treating others as he would wish to be treated. Continuously striving to enrich the financial literacy of his clients, David regularly disseminates invaluable insights through a widely subscribed weekly newsletter. To join the community of subscribers benefiting from his expertise, simply reach out to Connect@ClientsExcel.com.

Through his newsletter, David endeavors to provide actionable insights tailored to fortify your retirement preparations. Beyond the realm of financial planning, his aspiration is for clients to stride confidently into a stable financial future.

Beyond his professional pursuits, David finds joy and fulfillment in his role as a husband to Mallory and father to two young daughters,

Amelia and Ansley, alongside their cherished rescue dog, Oscar. Actively engaged in their Spartanburg church community, David has extended his passion for mentorship through involvement with Jump-Start, a ministry dedicated to supporting individuals transitioning from incarceration.

NOTES

Made in the USA
Columbia, SC
10 May 2025